Aquilla Books

This book is dedicated to my two wonderful children, whose creative input helped shape the ghastly characters you're about to meet.

This book belongs to:

_____

One Little Skeleton, Two Black Cats

A FUN AND SPOOKY COUNTING STORY

by

Donna Ostrom

1

One little skeleton
is rattling in the night.
He tumbles over a
pumpkin, and gives it
a big FRIGHT.

Two black cats
slip out to have some
fun. They scare the
poor skeleton
who then begins to run!

Three gory goblins
are giggling with glee.
They juggle with their
eyeballs...But OOPS!
Now they cannot see.

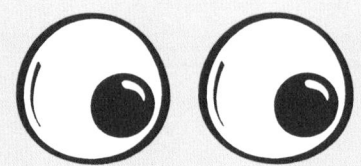

Four howling werewolves
sing songs to the full
moon.
Ouch! They really hurt
my ears! I hope they stop
singing soon.

Five wicked witches
on brooms begin to fly.
Listen to their cackles
as they zoooooom across
the sky.

Six ghoulish ghosties share a picnic in the park, until the littlest ghostie cries...
"But I'm afraid of the dark!"

7

Seven silly zombies
are playing hide and seek.
Shall we try to find them
and scare them with a
SHRIEK?

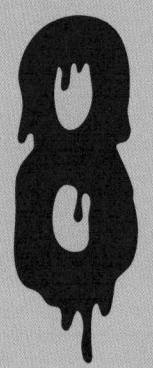

Eight mumbling mummies
moan and stomp around.
They slip in muddy
puddles
and fall to the ground.

Nine fat pumpkins
are lined up in a row.
See their scary faces
all spooky and aglow.

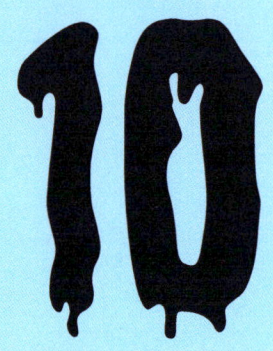

10

Ten little children
in costumes eerie and
bright, shout
TRICK OR TREAT
to all they meet
as they squeal with delight.

And all the spooky creatures,
each one ghastly and gory,

say HAPPY HALLOWEEN
to you, and hope you like
their story.

Also by Donna Ostrom

Mongoose Betty

Kristroff The Door Scratching Kitty

To keep up to date with new releases from the author, scan the QR code:

Published by Aquilla Books
Where stories are crafted with purpose
and told with pride

Aquilla Books

Printed in Dunstable, United Kingdom